First Day

🎺 Dominie Press, Inc.

Anna is going to school.
It is her first day.

Anna sees the bus.

She feels funny
in her tummy.

Anna sees other children.

She still feels funny
in her tummy.

Anna sees the school.

She still feels funny
in her tummy.

Anna sees her class
and her teacher, Mrs. Quick.

Anna still feels funny
in her tummy.

"Welcome, Anna!"
says Mrs. Quick.

Mrs. Quick says,
"Here is my bear, Zozo.
This is Zozo's first day.
Will you look after him?"

Anna looks after Zozo
at story time.

**Anna looks after Zozo
at art time.**

The other children help Anna to look after Zozo.

Anna goes out to play
with the other children.

"Oh!" says Anna.
"I forgot Zozo!"

"Zozo is fine," says Mrs. Quick.
"He has some new friends."

"I have some new friends, too,"
says Anna.